WINSTON CUP RACING

Sallie Stephenson

CRESTWOOD HOUSE
New York

Maxwell Macmillan Canada
Toronto

Maxwell Macmillan International
New York   Oxford   Singapore   Sydney

Copyright © 1991 by Crestwood House, Macmillan Publishing Company

Crestwood House
Macmillan Publishing Company
866 Third Avenue
New York, NY 10022

Maxwell Macmillan Canada, Inc.
1200 Eglinton Avenue East
Suite 200
Don Mills, Ontario M3C 3N1

Macmillan Publishing Company is part of the Maxwell Communication Group of Companies.

First edition

Printed in the United States of America

10 9 8 7 6 5 4 3 2 1

Stephenson, Sallie.
  Winston cup racing / by Sallie Stephenson.—1st ed.
      p.   cm.—(Fast track)
  Includes bibliographical references (p.) and index.
  Summary: A behind-the-scenes look at the Winston Cup series of stock car races, focusing on the Daytona 500.
  ISBN 0-89686-695-5
  1. Stock car racing—Juvenile literature. 2. Daytona International Speedway Race—Juvenile literature. [1.Stock car racing. 2. Daytona International Speedway Race.] I. Title.   II. Series: Stephenson, Sallie. Fast track.
GV1029.9.S74S745 1991
796.7'2—dc20
                                                                    91-11904

INTRODUCTION

SPOTLIGHT ON THE DRIVER

BEHIND THE SCENES

The Magic of Speed

Imagine that you are a fan sitting in the Daytona International Speedway grandstand waiting for the Daytona 500 to begin. Excitement charges the air as the cars sit side by side on the track, their drivers at the ready. The cars are Buicks, Chevys, Oldsmobiles, Fords and Pontiacs. Their body styles are just like the cars you see every day on the road. But these are no ordinary cars. And these are no ordinary drivers.

At last the sports announcer tells the drivers to start their engines. The roar fills your ears. You watch as the **pace car** leads the race cars around the track. You can feel the tension as the superpowered cars gain speed. When the pace car leaves the track, the green flag drops—and the race is on!

◀ Cars thunder around the track during a Winston Cup race.

There is a blur of colors and **sponsors'** decals as the cars roar past you. Soon the stock cars are reaching speeds of up to 180 miles per hour. The noise of the engines is so loud that you might want to wear earplugs. The sound *they* create is like a million angry wasps. *Mmmmrrrrmm! Mmmmrrrrmm! Mmmmrrrrmm!*

Danger is in the air. The cars are so close and are racing so fast that you're on the edge of your seat. Only inches separate them as the cars jockey for position, door to door and bumper to bumper. If one car touches another at the high speeds, the outcome can be dangerous. Just one slip by a driver can send the whole pack spinning in a multicar collision.

A driver may have to climb out of a heap of bent metal and smoking tires. But he or she would be lucky. Many times, crashes mean serious injury and death.

Finally, after hours of close calls and overheated engines, two cars barrel toward the finish line in a fight for first place. Is it Richard Petty, the king of stock car racing, roaring toward yet another victory? Is that Cale Yarborough alongside him? Or is it another racing star like Terry Labonte? This year, could a woman driver win the Daytona 500 for the first time? Or perhaps the winner is a **rookie** driver, competing for the first time in the Daytona 500.

Your throat is raw from shouting for your favorite, and you hold your breath as the engines howl and the fans scream.

This is the most thrilling part of the race. But let's take time out to see what lies behind the roar and excitement. Why would someone risk life and limb strapped into a smoking-hot, 3,500-pound superpowered hunk of metal hurtling 180 miles an hour? Before the winner crosses that finish line, let's look at the challenges and rewards of Winston Cup racing. Let's see why men and women get hooked on the magic of speed.

What Is Winston Cup Racing?

Winston Cup racing is the name given to a series of races. Probably the most famous race is the Daytona 500. This is the first of the 29 races in the Winston Cup series. These events take place all around the country. All of them involve stock cars racing on tracks of varying lengths and different shapes.

Stock cars are cars with standard, or stock, bodies that you can find at any auto dealership. But these racing vehicles have been totally built

Winston Cup race teams are sponsored by large companies like Kodak.

by hand, with special engines. They are capable of withstanding grueling races—some as long as four hours—at speeds up to 180 miles per hour. The Winston Cup series takes its name from Winston cigarettes, its sponsor.

At each race in the Winston Cup series, drivers are awarded points for how well they perform. The winner receives the most points, the second-place finisher fewer points, and so on. These drivers compete in many races during the racing season. At each race they earn more points. At the end of the racing season, the driver who has earned the most points gains the title of Winston Cup champion. This means that the driver has performed better than any other in all of the Winston Cup races combined.

Behind the Wheel

The first time you sit in a race car and hear the engine fire up, the noise pulsates through the car. You can feel it charge your whole body. The sound actually builds up your level of excitement. You might be tempted to think that all you need to do to win is to drive as fast as you possibly can. But any veteran driver will tell you that driving a race car involves much more than putting your foot to the floorboard.

Good eye-to-hand coordination and the ability to judge distance are musts for a race car driver. At high speeds, the driver has to be able to brake, shift gears and **accelerate**. A good driver must know how his or her racing machine works and how to handle it for the best results.

Physical endurance is important. The Daytona 500 is so named for the amount of miles the cars need to travel to win. The race takes about four hours even at top speeds. By contrast, a drag race is over in seconds! And while a drag race takes place with only 2 cars racing against each other on a straightaway, a race like the Daytona 500 always has at least 32 cars battling for first place on a track with banked curves.

On such a track the ability to make split-second decisions is critical. Of course, risk taking is part of racing. But the risks are not as great if the driver has a ready plan of action based on what might happen during the race. A driver has to consider **pit stops**, tire changes and other factors that cause delays.

Always, the driver must have courage and nerve. Often he or she has to rise above fear and perform perfectly in the face of great danger. In fact, mental attitude is perhaps most important to success. A good race driver thinks positively and is intensely competitive. If there's one thing all drivers have in common, it is the desire to be the best, no matter what it takes.

During a pit stop, the race crew may change a tire or fix any problems that have come up during the race.

Inside the Stock Car

Although a stock car looks like an ordinary automobile, it isn't the sort of car you'd want to take on a Sunday outing! It lacks comfortable upholstery. It has no passenger seats. The cockpit is the driver's "office." The left side of the cockpit holds the driver's seat. A steel frame in the shape of a tube protects the driver on all sides. It's a snug fit.

The front windshield is glass. The rest of the windows are hard plastic. There is no window on the driver's side. There is only a net through which a tube can be inserted so he or she can get a drink.

Two crash bars crisscross the middle of the car. They are welded to **roll bars** at the car's **fire wall**. They extend across the roof behind the driver's head. These help prevent the driver from being crushed if the car flips over.

The dashboard is simple but functional.

11

Inside a stock car

Directly facing the driver are four gauges that monitor water temperature, oil temperature, oil pressure and amount of fuel. There is also a **tachometer**, which records **engine rpms**. When the engine oil pressure falls too low, a warning light goes on.

A two-way radio is mounted on the door closest to the driver so that he or she can talk to the crew chief. The crew chief can alert the driver to any dangers on the track and can advise the driver when to make a pit stop.

There are several safety features in the car. A fire extinguisher is within easy reach. All the driver has to do is pull a cable and hit the plunger to make it spray. And the gas tank is specially designed to prevent a fire from breaking out in the event of a collision.

On the car's right-hand side are two metal boxes instead of a passenger seat. One holds the oil tank. The other is called the cool-suit box because it holds a block of ice. Two oil coolers, one on each side, are mounted where the backseat would be in an ordinary car. The ignition system is mounted inside the car with the driver, instead of under the hood, to keep it as cool as possible.

There are also special tires on a stock car. They are large racing tires, and they have no tread, or grooves. They are made of a special **compound** that grips the track and helps the race car go faster.

Stock cars have a **spoiler** on the rear deck. A spoiler is a metal strip that makes the car go faster and keeps the car close to the track when moving at very high speeds.

Track temperatures become so hot that the temperature inside the car can rise above 120 degrees Fahrenheit. The tires may reach temperatures of over 200 degrees Fahrenheit! The engine's exhaust pipe runs right under the floor, which heats up the car even more. Heat-resistant padding under the seat helps, but there is no air-conditioning unit in a race car.

Carbon-monoxide fumes well up in the cockpit. Breathing the vapors can make a person very tired. Drivers have been known to collapse when they get out of their cars.

You can imagine how exhausting it must be to race for four hours in the heat and discomfort of a stock car!

Before the Race

Before a race like the Daytona 500, a driver and crew are busy getting ready. The race car must conform to rules set by the National Association for Stock Car Auto Racing, or NASCAR for short.

A crew inspects a car before a race.

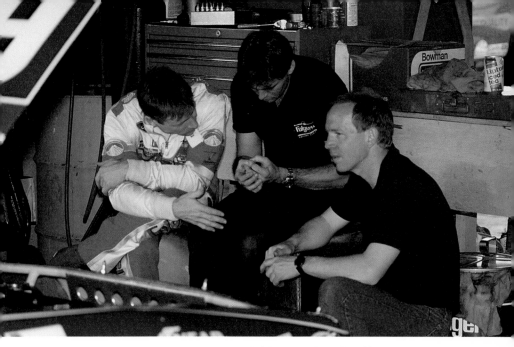
Before a race the driver and his mechanic discuss any problems that might occur during the race.

When the driver, the crew and the owner arrive at the track, they sign in. The race car transporter is parked in a special area of the garage. The transporter carries the race car and one or more extra engines, in addition to a complete machine shop with spare tires.

Few people besides the driver, the crew and the owner of the team are allowed into the garage area. That is where the race car and the equipment are unloaded.

To prepare for inspection, the car is elevated on four jack stands. The front wheels are removed to make it easier to get to the motor.

Next, parts such as the **carburetor** are removed to make sure that they conform to NASCAR rules.

A team may sometimes try to bend the rules a bit to get a better edge. The crew might try to load extra fuel by pumping gas into the car's roll bars or some other well-hidden place. If the inspectors find the extra gas, the team may be fined.

Different NASCAR inspectors look at different parts of the race car. There are a number of inspections. The final inspection is at the weight scales. A competing car must weigh 3,500 pounds before it is allowed to qualify, or enter a race. If it is under this weight, then the crew has to add enough lead to reach the required weight.

Before it is weighed, the car is filled with gasoline. Then it is weighed without the driver. More than once a helmet with extra lead in it has been left in the driver's seat to add weight to a car that was too light. NASCAR inspectors are on the lookout for this kind of cheating.

After the car is weighed, it is pushed back to the garage to be prepared for the first practice session. The car is started and allowed to reach the right operating temperature. A new set of tires is put on. The crew checks and double-checks the car. Finally it's time for a practice run.

Driving the Track

The driver slides into the race car and adjusts the seat and shoulder belts, if necessary. He or she is wearing a racing helmet, which has to fit certain safety standards, as well as fireproof clothing, including underwear, gloves and shoes. The driver quickly adjusts the rearview mirror and steps on the brake to check that it's working. Then he or she starts the car and checks the gauges to make sure the engine reaches the right water and oil temperatures.

During a practice session, the driver pulls out on the track to see how the car handles. He or she wants to run on the inside, or the lowest part, of the banked track in the turns to get the fastest time. The crew chief tells the driver by

A crew pushes a car into position on the track for a practice session.

way of the radio what the lap time is as the car roars around the track. The lap time is the time in seconds that it takes to go once around the track. As the lap time gets faster, the driver moves up the track. He or she stays in the **groove** where the fastest time is clocked.

As the driver goes, he or she checks any vibrations, shakes or rattles that may turn into problems later on. The driver usually does two or three hard laps around the track.

When the practice is over, the driver discusses with the crew chief in detail the way the car handled. Then the crew makes changes in the car.

A record is kept of how the race car is "set up." A setup chart is filled out to record measurements. The chart is full of technical terms, such as **caster**, **camber** and **tire pressure**.

The next time the race car runs at this track, the car will be set up the same way. Most team owners have at least two race cars. They might look the same on the outside, but they are set up differently, depending on the track each one will run on. For example, the track at Richmond, Virginia, is short. A car will be set up one way for a short track and another way for a **superspeedway** such as Daytona.

After the setup record has been made, the car is ready for the next important step on the road to victory.

Qualifying Rounds

In order to decide who will race and in which position on the track, NASCAR officials hold **qualifying rounds**. The qualifying rounds are held in two sessions. On the first day, the 20 fastest cars qualify. Those racers who are left compete in the second session on the following day. Some starting positions are better than others. The best position is number one, which is also called the "pole" position. The cars race two abreast in about 20 rows. The number one position is in the first row on the side closest to the infield, the area in the center of the track. The track is open during the qualifying rounds, so many fans are able to watch.

Before the rounds, the race car is pushed to an inspection station. The inspectors open the hood and check for a carburetor seal. If the seal has not been broken, the hood is sealed and cannot be opened. The car again goes to the scales. It goes to the gas pumps to get enough gas to bring it to legal weight. Then it is pushed to the pit road, the starting place on the track.

Once the car is on the line, nothing can be done to it unless permission is given by an official. Now winning is up to the driver.

Alone on the track, the driver tries to achieve his or her very fastest lap time. It would be ter-

In a race like the Daytona 500, drivers compete fiercely for good starting positions.

rifying and dangerous for a driver to actually drive a whole race this fast. The competition is fierce for the chance to race on the big day. In order to earn the pole position, the driver must drive faster than all the others.

Hazards

No matter how well a car performs, success or failure often rests only with how quickly and well a driver can react.

You're turning. You're trying to get the car straightened out. Then, unexpectedly, you hit a slick spot on the track.

You spin out. The brakes lock momentarily. You're probably wondering if you'll be hit on the side, or broadsided. This fear races through your mind even as you're spinning. If the car is out of control, the right thing to do is to put your foot hard on the brakes. This is called "standing on the brakes." You hold on to the steering wheel until you come to a stop. Then you put the car into first gear. You look around to see where you are and what's happening around you. After that you can get back in the race.

This time you were lucky.

You didn't wreck the car. You managed to stay out of an accident. But next time you might not be so lucky.

When a car is out of control, the driver must make an immediate plan of action and hope that he or she is right. A crash can happen so fast that the driver doesn't have time to react. It's over in a matter of a second or two. Fortunately, cars are built better today than they used to be. They can usually take a head-on crash against the wall. The driver often can walk away from even a bad crash.

One of the worst things that can happen in a stock car is to be broadsided—T-boned, the drivers call it. This happens when you get hit on the driver's side by another car. The great Bobby Allison was killed at Pocono Speedway in 1988 when this happened to his car.

Two main challenges a driver must face on

the track are how to control the car when it is **pushing** and when it is **loose**.

In stock car lingo, a race car is pushing when it tries to go straight instead of turning. When it is pushing, an experienced driver won't try to muscle the car to make it go around the turns. Wrestling with the wheel usually causes the car to go toward the wall.

When the rear end of the car swings around and seems to be trying to pass its front end, the car has another problem. Then it is said to be loose. This is often caused by too much front-end weight or springs that are too stiff.

A driver's crew can make changes that will help to control push and looseness. Loosening up the springs may help. Changing the **stagger** of the tires can also help make a car easier to handle. The crew may add more air to the tires on one side of the car. Since stock cars always run left, or counterclockwise, around the track, the left side of the car is made heavier to make it handle better.

Drafting is a way of getting a free tow during a race. It was first used by the famous driver Fireball Roberts at the Daytona International Speedway. When drafting, a car moves to with-

▶ In drafting, a racer follows the car in front of her very closely to take advantage of the air flow created by high speeds.

In a high-speed race a driver must watch out for his own safety as well as the safety of the other racers.

in inches of the car in front of it so that a suction effect is created. A pocket of air is formed just behind the first car. If the following driver can get the front of his car into this pocket, his car will be pulled along. At high speeds of at least 170 miles per hour, the speeds of both cars are increased. There may be as many as ten to twelve cars running nose-to-tail.

If you are drafting and there are cars on either side of you, you can really feel the pull. The vibrations caused by the air currents shake you, and you feel as if you're going to be pulled apart. But if you go along with it, you will be all right.

A Driver's Responsibilities

No driver wants to cause an accident in which another driver is injured or killed. A driver has a responsibility to be well trained before he or she enters a race.

Many races are held on long superspeedway tracks, such as the one at Daytona. The speeds at which the cars travel there are twice as fast as the speeds reached on shorter tracks. So the driver has to think about speed at every moment. If the car comes into a pit stop too fast, it can endanger people's lives.

A pit crew makes an adjustment to a car's engine during the Daytona 500.

In fact, pit stops can be nearly as dangerous as the track itself. The cars drive frantically into the pits. The drivers know that every second counts. They have to find their crew in the blur of pit signs. There may be 20 cars in the same general area at the same time. The crew scrambles over the walls with new tires and gas. Pit stops generally take only 15 to 20 *seconds*!

The crew members swarm around the car like bees. NASCAR rules allow only six people over the wall to service each car. One cleans the windshield. Two pour gas. One jacks up the car. Two change tires. A good crew can change two outside tires and refuel in only 12 or 13 seconds. Longer races may have as many as six tire changes, so it is important to do them as fast as possible. Teamwork is crucial. Many of the crews have been together for years.

Getting into Stock Car Racing

Breaking into racing takes money—yours or someone else's. The more money, the more successful the operation.

It can cost as much as $50,000 a week to be a stock car racer. A brand-new driver has a problem. No backer, or sponsor, wants to give him or her money because there's no proof that the driver can win. The driver may have to be his or her own sponsor at first. Then the driver is called an **independent**. Such drivers often have to make do with secondhand parts and tires.

Even drivers who have been racing for years have problems getting sponsors to help pay for having a car built, a crew to maintain it, and all the other expenses of racing. All of these things are very expensive. For example, an engine can cost as much as $25,000, and most engines are rebuilt between races. A driver must show proven ability to get a sponsor to commit to a career.

Having a sponsor allows a racer to pay all the expenses associated with supporting a car and race crew.

The Day of the Race

On the day of the race, the track opens at 6:30 A.M. The cars go through inspection again. Then they are fueled before being pushed into line on the pit road. The pits are set up with equipment, spare parts and tools.

The drivers arrive at the track about 10 A.M. At 11 o'clock there is a drivers' meeting, during which rules are discussed. (Sometimes a rookies' meeting is held three or four days before the race so that new drivers can get the chance to ask questions.)

The drivers then suit up, and the cars are given their last-minute checks. Finally a voice booms over the public-address system: "Start your engines."

The cars warm up. Then the officials signal the drivers onto the track. Communications between driver and crew chief are checked. The drivers follow the pace car. The pace car

The crowd in the packed grandstand watches as cars race around the track at the Daytona International Speedway.

goes around the track a couple of times to bring all the cars up to speeds of about 100 miles per hour.

Now the green flag drops. The race is on!

The attention of the fans is all on the drivers. But even on the day of a race, many other people behind the scenes play important roles. Who are they?

The owner of the race team stands on top of the transport truck that brought the car to the track. During the race he looks for trouble on the track. He radios any information to the crew chief and the driver.

The crew chief works closely with the driver

all during the race. The crew chief is the number one boss on the track. The crew members follow his or her orders.

Spotters are out along the track. They radio information about the track to the crew chief.

On the loudspeaker, the announcer tells the fans what is happening during the race.

NASCAR officials are busy too. They go up and down the pit road, looking for problems. They may impose a penalty on a rule offender.

The flagman is in a stand by the track. When he signals the drivers with a green flag, he's telling them to race. When he waves a yellow caution flag, he's advising them to leave the track. He also signals when the race is over.

The pit crew gases up a car during a pit stop.

The checkered flag falls as the winner crosses the finish line.

The pace car driver's job isn't done after the first laps. He or she also comes out on the track whenever the yellow caution flag is out.

There is also a track physician. The doctor gives each of the drivers a physical examination at the start of the racing season and takes care of any injuries during each race. There is a center at the track for medical emergencies.

Journalists are located in the press box. They have a good view of the race and report the details to newspapers and radio and television stations.

Don't forget the concession-stand workers.

What fun would it be to watch a race without hot dogs and soda?

Last but not least are the ticket sellers. If they didn't sell the fans tickets, no one could see the drivers compete!

Besides all these people, there are others who paved the way. Without the pioneers of racing, the sport wouldn't be what it is today. You might be surprised to learn how it all began.

The Start of It All

Long before there was a multimillion-dollar superspeedway at Daytona, there was racing at the beach. It began nearly a hundred years ago, in the early 1900s. Almost as soon as automobiles were invented, people started wondering how fast they could go.

It started on a 23-mile-long strip of hard-packed white sand lying alongside the Atlantic Ocean. Early automobile racers took a "flying start" to build up speed before attempting to clock the fastest speed over a measured distance of one mile.

The first international speed trials were held at Ormond-Daytona Beach in Florida in 1904. William K. Vanderbilt, a millionaire sportsman, drove his gasoline-powered Mercedes to a world-record speed of 92.303 miles per hour. In 1927 Sir Henry Segrave became the first to reach 200 miles per hour. He was a British race car driver who drove an English-made Sunbeam.

In 1935 another Englishman, Sir Malcolm Campbell, attained a speed of 276.816 miles per hour in his Bluebird. The long, sleek Bluebird was the most famous car to run on the beach. Inside the race car Campbell had a **cross site** trained on a huge target on the beach. He needed this device to guide him so that he didn't wander off course. The spectators in the grandstand saw a blur. Then they heard a sound like a clap of thunder. There was a path of swirling

In the early days of stock car racing, races were held along beaches. Here, a "pit crew" tries to rescue Curtis "Crawfish" Crider's car from the incoming tide.

sand. Then a big, blue ball of flame hung in midair for a second when Campbell cut the throttle.

After Sir Malcolm Campbell had made his run in 1935, the contests for speed on the sand were moved to the Bonneville Salt Flats, in Utah. This was a safer location for such high speeds. Most land-speed tests have been held there ever since. But what happened to Daytona Beach when the speed trials left?

The First Speedway

Many people in Daytona worried that, without the speed trials, Daytona Beach would become a racing ghost town. To preserve the racing tradition, city officials constructed a 3.2-mile-long beach and road course. The course was made from the original beach course, using an **asphalt** road that ran parallel to it. Curves were cut through the sand dunes to connect the straightaways. Stock car races were run on this oval-shaped sand-and-asphalt track for the next 20 years.

During the race, the cars would run two miles north on the wide, hard-packed sand of the Atlantic Ocean beach, slide sideways as

Early racers take the South Turn on the original Daytona
Beach track.

they approached the North Turn, then roar
through the short, man-made stretch of crushed
shell and sand. After that, they would race on
to the two-lane blacktop asphalt of South
Atlantic Avenue, continue for two miles down
to the South Turn, take another left to the beach
and then roar back up the course.

Mother Nature would determine what the
beach would be like. A northeast wind might
be ideal, creating a smooth beach for racing. A
west wind might make it bumpy. But no matter
what the condition of the course, it was always
exciting for both the drivers and the spectators.

The narrow North Turn was the scene of many crashes. At the other end of the course, the South Turn was hazardous too. Sometimes cars went over the outside bank, beyond the end of the stands, and slid across the beach and into the ocean. Fortunately, the grandstands at both turns were set back far enough so that the cars wouldn't endanger spectators. Hundreds of racing fans lined the dunes along the two-mile stretch of beach as well.

Stock car racing now had speed, fans and excitement. What it needed was organization and vision. It took one special man to make the sport what it is today.

The Man Who Created Stock Car Racing

Bill France came to Daytona in 1934 during the Depression. Many people were broke and jobs were scarce. He was on his way from Washington, D.C., to Miami to make a new home with his wife and baby son. In Daytona his car broke down. He had only $25 in his pocket and $75 back in a bank in Washington. Lacking enough money to fix his car, Bill

France and his family decided to stay in Daytona. He liked the beach, and he could find a job and fix the car himself with his own tools.

He got a job at first as a mechanic. He later opened his own service station. He liked to race cars, and when Daytona Beach sponsored its first stock car event in 1936, France drove his car to a fifth-place finish. He continued to compete for the next several years.

Stock car racing was just starting to become popular as a sporting event. Soon France realized that he could make more money arranging and promoting the racers than actually racing in them. In December 1947 he called a special meeting. He invited racing promoters, drivers, car builders, car owners, mechanics and prominent racing enthusiasts.

Out of this meeting the National Association for Stock Car Auto Racing was born. Bill France became its first president. From this time on, NASCAR would establish racing procedures

The start of the 1949 Daytona Beach race

and regulations. NASCAR would give the sport the respectability it needed.

In the early days of NASCAR, the cars that ran in the races were not machines of great beauty. They were cars without fenders. They were "souped up," with high-power engines that made them go faster. They were also outdated models. Then Bill France had another idea.

The Grand Nationals

In 1949 Bill France figured out a way to draw attention to NASCAR and build its reputation. He guessed that instead of watching older cars, fans would like to see automobiles that looked just like the ones they drove. He was right.

France formed a special racing division for late-model automobiles. These events were called the Grand National races. This name was kept until the 1980s, when R. J. Reynolds, the tobacco company, became the sponsor of the series. The Grand Nationals were renamed the Winston Cup series, after the cigarettes of that tobacco company.

The first late-model stock car race was held in Charlotte, North Carolina, on June 19, 1949.

A record-breaking crowd of 18,000 people attended. Eight more Grand National races were held that year. Stock car racing had entered the major leagues.

After NASCAR was formed and the Grand National races began, stock car competition became more and more popular. Racing tracks all over the country started drawing larger crowds.

Today each driver who competes in a NASCAR Winston Cup race is awarded national championship points. At the end of the racing year, which ends in November, a victory dinner is held. A $1 million prize is given to the driver who has scored the most points during the year. This is in addition to the regular salary the driver receives plus his share of the winnings for each race. Every driver wins some money in a race. But the top driver earns the most.

Daytona International Speedway

Back in 1949 Bill France still wasn't finished dreaming. Soon he had another idea: a plan for

The superspeedway at Daytona

a superspeedway in Daytona Beach. He wanted to build a huge stadium that would hold many more fans than the beach-to-road track did.

France had seen the superspeedway track that had been built near Darlington, South Carolina, in 1949. It was a 1 1/4-mile oval track with a grandstand in which 9,000 people could sit and watch the races. The first 500-mile stock car race, the Southern 500, had been held at Darlington, and a crowd of 30,000 had come out to watch it. Why couldn't an even bigger track be built in Daytona?

Bill France chose 470 acres of land on Daytona's west side. He worked hard to raise money to finance the project. It was a big job.

Daytona International Speedway opened in 1959. It had taken more than $3 million to build it.

The superspeedway is built in a D-shaped tri-oval. This gives the track three turns instead of the two an oval track has. The three turns are sharply raised at the outer edges. This "banking" permits cars to take the corners faster.

Along the north side of the track nine permanent grandstands were built. Here more than 90,000 fans can cheer for their favorite drivers. Each grandstand at Daytona International Speedway is named after a well-known racer of the past: Sir Malcolm Campbell, Sir Henry Segrave, Barney Oldfield, Ray Keech, Ralpha DePalma, Joe Weatherly and Fireball Roberts.

At the center of the race track is a grassy area called the **infield.** More than one million cubic yards of dirt were removed from the infield to build the high-banked turns. This created a man-made lake—Lake Lloyd.

The infield holds 50,000 spectators and cars. A road course where sports cars and motorcycles can race cuts through the infield. It is 3.56 miles in length. A 250-foot tunnel under the race track allows vehicles to enter and exit the infield.

When the Daytona International Speedway opened, it was the finest racing facility for stock cars in the country. Today it is one of the busiest racing centers in the United States. The speedway has its own security bureau, maintenance staff, fire department, ambulance corps and a first-rate, eight-bed medical care center.

The Big D is used about 65 percent of the year for races and tests. Each year two NASCAR Winston Cup races are held there—the Daytona 500 in February and the Firecracker 400 every July 4.

In February over 500,000 fans attend Speed Weeks at the Big D. During Speed Weeks a series of races are held for different classes of racing cars. The Daytona 500 is the highlight and concluding event of Speed Weeks. This event draws some of the best stock cars and the best stock car drivers in the country.

Victory

Let's go back to the grandstands at the Daytona 500. You're on your feet now, your eyes glued to the two cars hurtling toward the finish line in a blast of heat and smoke and snarling horsepower. The fans send up a roar that rattles the bleachers as your favorite driver suddenly pulls ahead. It's a win by only two feet!

The winning team celebrates after a race.

You cheer as the flag waves your driver to victory. But now you know you're cheering for more than one driver or one event. Behind every stock car race lies a thrilling story of risk taking, vision and the courage of champions.

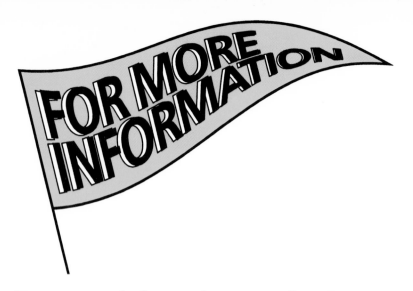

For more information on the Daytona International Speedway and Winston Cup racing, write to:

Larry Balewski
Public Relations Director
Daytona International Speedway
1801 Volusia Avenue
Daytona Beach, FL 32114-1243

or:

Curtis W. Crider
1077 Roberts Street
Ormond Beach, FL 32074

FOR FURTHER READING

Chapin, Kim. *The Story of Stock Car Racing: Fast as White Lightning*. New York: The Dial Press, 1981.

Crider, Curtis "Crawfish," as told to Don O'Reilly. *The Road to Daytona*. Ormond Beach, FL: Self-published, 1987.

Dolder, Bill. *Stock Car Racing*. New York: Gallery Books, 1990.

Higdon, Hal. *Showdown at Daytona*. New York: G. P. Putnam's Sons, 1976.

Krishef, Robert K. *The Daytona 500*. Minneapolis, MN: Lerner Publications Co., 1976.

Manning, Skip. *How to Go Grand National Racing*. Santa Ana, CA: Steve Smith Autosports, 1979.

Neely, William. *Daytona USA*. Tucson, AZ: Aztex, 1979.

GLOSSARY/INDEX

lines stay on the target, the driver will not wander off course.

drafting 22, 24—When two or more cars run nose-to-tail, almost touching. The second car is pulled along by the pocket of air formed behind the first car.

engine rpms 12—Engine revolutions per minute.

fire wall 11—The structural wall between the driver and the engine.

groove 18—The path around the race track that a driver thinks is the fastest for him or her. The "high groove" takes a car closer to the outside wall for most of a lap. The "low groove" takes a car closer to the infield.

independent 27—A driver who has no sponsor. He or she has to pay the expenses of racing, which can be very costly.

infield 41—The central area enclosed by the race track.

looseness 22—A handling problem in which the rear of the car wants to swing around, as though it were trying to catch up to the front.

pace car 5, 28, 31—An automobile that leads the competitors in the first lap but does not actually compete. It sets an even speed for the beginning of the race.

pit stop 10, 25, 26—A stop for food, fuel, rest or relief during an automobile race.

pushing 22—A racing car's tendency to plow toward the wall.

qualifying rounds 19—Competitions to determine which drivers will be allowed to race and in which starting positions. One car at a time does a single, timed lap around the track. The fastest car gets the best starting position, the next fastest gets second position, and so on.

roll bar 11—The steel bar in a race car that protects the driver in a turnover.

rookie 6—A first-year Winston Cup driver.

spoiler 13—A metal strip on a race car that helps it go faster. The front spoiler is found underneath the car's front end; the rear spoiler is attached to the trunk lid.

sponsor 6, 27—A person or business that pays expenses for a racing team in return for advertising.

stagger 22—The difference in size between the tires on the left side of the car and the tires on the right.

superspeedway 18—A race track over one mile in length.

tachometer 12—An instrument that tells the driver how fast the car engine is turning over.

tire pressure 18—Pressure of air in a tire measured in pounds per square inch.